# COPYRIGHT NOTICE

This publication is protected under the US Copyright Act of 1976 and all other applicable international, federal, state and local laws, and all rights are reserved, including resale rights. You are not allowed to give or sell this publication to anyone else.

If you received this publication from anyone other than the author; Jahangir Alam Jony then you've received a pirated copy. Please contact at "**jonyalamonlinestore@gmail.com**" and notify us of the situation. There may be a reward!

Please note that much of this publication is based on personal experience and anecdotal evidence. Although the author has made every reasonable attempt to achieve complete accuracy of the content in this guide, he assumes no responsibility for any errors or omissions.

Also, you should use this information as you see it, and at your own risk. Your particular situation may not be exactly suited to the examples illustrated here; in fact, it's likely that they won't be the same, and you should adjust your use of the information and recommendations accordingly.

Any trademarks, service marks, product names or other legal designations are assumed to be the property of their respective owners, and are used only for reference.

The use of these terms does not imply any endorsement.

# WHY I WROTE THIS BOOK

*Search Engine Optimization is the very effective way to promote your products or service to the millions of customers online. It is your most shortcut path for promoting the products on the net. With a little help from the Search Engines, you can get thousands of relevant traffic or buyers on your website. But it is a matter of great regret that if you are quite new in online world then there is only few ways to learn the exactly formula how you can master the search engines optimization and be on top of the results within very short-time.*

*Also, don't have anything to promote? Don't have your own products or service? Fine you can work as an SEO optimizer on many freelancing site & can earn lots of money from it. For picturing each and every thing about SEO & how you can use it, to make a full living. Thinking about all these I create this book. By finishing it, you can master the search engine very quickly & can earn some real money from it.*

*When I start my online journey it took me years to find the exactly method, the proven strategy to do SEO and rank my website. Before finding that I do a lots of courses, buy a lots of book but it doesn't make any sense. As a beginner I struggle a lot to learn the SEO & all its component. So, I don't want you to do the same mistakes buying a lots of books and courses what doesn't make any sense. Follow me and my most proven techniques to master Google and others search engines and dominate the ranking factors.*

*Search Engine Optimization (SEO) is used in all aspects of web marketing. You need to understand as much as you can about how SEO works in order to get the proper marketing of your website online when you are promoting yourself (your own products or service) or promoting others products to earn a commission. I write this book for those people who have their own products but doesn't know where they can promote it. Also, especially for those people who doesn't have a product of their own but still wanted to make an online marketing platform.*

*For the people who doesn't have any products I introduce Clickbank and others affiliate marketplace from where you can select a product and promote that on the foundation we will learn to create on this book. Whenever you sell a product you can earn a commission for that particular sell. It is great isn't it? Clickbank is the best affiliate marketplace from where we can generate tons of sell. For introducing and using the Clickbank affiliate program and turning our campaigns into a money making machine I introduce this book to you.*

*For walking through together step by step, selecting a promising and convertible product. Building a SEO friendly website for advertising our selected product. Learning all the SEO components for ranking our website & drive relevant high quality traffic into the affiliate offers for making a sell.*

*For clearing all these essential steps, I create "SEO+Clickbank" so that you can earn some real money by using the opportunity the online marketplace already created for you. Myself, I also create a strong foundation by fully following what you can make hundreds, thousands of sells/month & earn huge amounts of cash from your affiliate commission. It's a full proven method. Step by step process, so follow it & enjoy the success.*

*The main target of creating this book is to give you the full blueprint I use for ranking a website. You can learn about both SEO & Affiliate Marketplace. How you use both of them combined & build a very strong foundation for making a full living. It's specially created for the beginners & the people who are struggling to be successful on online marketplace.*

*I am also giving you a full guide how you can build a website, that will save hundreds and thousands of dollars. If you wanted to do freelancing, then use all the SEO knowledge I am giving you thought out this book and apply those strategies into the client's website you would like to rank. I am 100% sure that you can rank any website with 1-3 month if you apply the strategy I am giving you by my book. Thanks for buying my book and getting started. I am so excited to teach you all the things I know. Hope you are also very excited too. So, without wasting any time let's learn "SEO+Clickbank". Best of luck!!!!*

# WHAT WE WILL COVER IN THIS BOOK

* Introduction of Search Engine Optimization.

* Tech the Search Engine Optimization from a beginner level.

* Picture Each & Every Topics Related to SEO.

* Introducing the Affiliate Marketplace.

* Clickbank Marketplace & How to Open an Account.

* Picking Up A product.

* How to Build a Website.

* How to Make Your Website SEO Friendly.

* Turn Your Website into Money Making Machine.

* Optimize Content for Your Website.

* Social Media Presence in SEO.

* Earn a Little More Money by Advertising.

* Introduction of the Google AdSense.

* How We Can Earn Huge Money by Using Google PPC.

* Drive Traffic to Your Website.

* Convert Traffic into Sells & Visitors into Customer.

And many more....

# About The Author

Jahangir Alam Jony is one of the most noticeable upcoming young SEO Experts & Affiliate Marketer. He is also a well-known web designer as well. At the very early of his age, he established himself solidly in the online world. First created his website on local market when he was just 14 years old. In 2006 he combined his website with Clickbank and started advertising various products.

He runs a couple of successful Google AdWords campaign and earns a lots of cash from it. He is a master of Email Marketing. In SEO, he has an in-depth knowledge of the Search Engines & their algorithms. Nowadays he is the most shortcut way of ranking your website in Google or Bing.

Blogging is another part of his passion. He has already made lots of blog or website for the clients what is dominating the Google at present. But Jahangir Alam Jony is most well-known for his heart-breathing writing. Unique, informative & reader-friendly content makes him one of the most favorite writer in his local market. Now he is on Amazon. So, you can expect a new book in each & every month from him.

Consistency & hard work is the core of this young writer's success. He is a big fan of Amazon Kindle & that's why he is here to share his knowledge & experience with you. His inexpensive book will help you within your journey on the online marketplace if you would like to establish yourself *on the net. Follow his proven methods & techniques for building a solid foundation for yourself. Buy his book and add your name to the successful online marketer's lists. I hope you will enjoy his writing.*

## *Reference Book;*

1. *Page One Ranking Factor*
2. *Search Engine Optimization for WordPress*
3. *Blogging for Dummies*
4. *How to Build a Website for Dummies*

# TABLE OF CONTENT

## Table of Contents

Copyright Notice ................................................................ 1

Why I Wrote This Book ...................................................... 2

What we will cover in this book ........................................ 5

About The Author ............................................................... 6

Table of content ................................................................. 9

Chapter 1 - What Is Search Engine Optimization? ......... 10

CHAPTER 2 - How SEARCH ENGINE works? ................ 16

CHAPTER 3 – Understanding the full on page search engine ranking factor. .................................................... 20

CHAPTER 4 – Understanding the full off page search engine ranking factor. .................................................... 34

CHAPTER 5 – Introducing Clickbank & selecting our product. ............................................................................. 41

CHAPTER 6 – Brainstorming the Keywords. ................. 47

CHAPTER 7 – Forecast Future Earning. ......................... 53

Chapter 8 – Picking & Set Up Domain+Hosting ............ 56

Chapter 9 – Design Your Website .................................. 62

Chapter 10 – Turn Your Website Into Money Making matchine ........................................................................... 71

Chapter 11- Start Advertising More Products & Earn little more Money ............................................................ 81

Chapter 12- How to Drive Easy & Quality Traffic in Your Website ............................................................................. 97

Chapter 13- Finish Line & Time for Say Good BYE ..... 125

# Chapter 1 - What Is Search Engine Optimization?

Search Engine Optimization (SEO) is used in all aspects of web marketing. You need to understand as much as you can about how SEO works in order to get the proper marketing of your website online.

When you use SEO in all of your content - both text and visual, you can draw more traffic to your site. In order to understand how to use SEO, you need to know why people use this type of marketing and rely on it so heavily in order to get the desired traffic to their website. SEO is what gets a website noticed in the search engines.

So what exactly is SEO? This sets up your text, photos and videos so that they are easy to find when someone is searching for them using the various search engines online. While it is often said that Google relies more on SEO content than Yahoo, which relies more on link building, the truth of the matter is that in order for a website to be discovered online, it must come up in the search engine.

For example, if you have a website that sells cooking appliances, you will want to make sure that you structure your site so that others who may be looking for the products you sell will be able to find it online. Those who are looking online for what you have to sell may do it in a number of different ways, although the easiest way for someone to find something online is to use the search engines. Most of the traffic to your website will come from search engine optimization.

You need to know which keywords will work for your website. These are the words or phrases that people will put into the search engine bars to receive the search engine results pages. Many people today are putting in longer phrases into the search engines to narrow down their search.

There are tools that the website owner can use to investigate the best keywords for their website, based on what they sell and what words potential customers are likely to plug into the search bars that will lead them to the site. In order to succeed at this, a website owner must not only know the concept of SEO, but also much about the target market, which is those who are most likely to purchase the products on the website.

If you are just starting out your website, or if you have a website up and running already, you need to know how to use search engine optimization in all facets of your marketing. While there are other ways to market your website and products without using SEO, the fact of the matter is that 60 percent of all traffic on websites comes from those who found the website in the search engines. These people are seeking out what you have to offer and are finding you online as long as you are accessible.

Once your site is search engine optimized, you can expect to get more traffic to your site from the search engines. People who may be interested in your site will find it easier if your website is search engine optimized. Most people use the search engines to find what they are looking for when they go online. By having your website optimized and easy to find in the search engine results pages, you can attract more traffic to your website through the search engines.

There are many internet marketing companies that will help you get your website search engine optimized and keep it that way. Some of the methods that they use to optimize a website include the following:

- Article marketing
- Blogs
- Press Releases
- Video ads
- Google ads

All of these can be optimized in order to incorporate keywords that will make the website appear in the search engine results pages or, in the case of Google ads, land them on pages where they are most likely to find people who will be interested in your website. The entire purpose of making a website search engine optimized is to make it easier for potential clients or customers to visit your site.

Those who may be interested in your products or services can only take advantage of them if the know about them and where to get them. You have, most likely, gone on line in search of something that you wanted to buy at one time or another. Chances are that you put the information into the search engine toolbar to pull up search engine results pages. You probably sifted through a few pages before you came up with what you wanted.

This is the basic concept of SEO. Those who understand how to use SEO to make their website more searchable and likely to come up in the first two pages of the search engine results pages are more likely to have clients land on their site.

There are probably many sites out there that offer you interesting information as well as products or services. Unfortunately, many of them are buried deep in the search engine results pages.

Most people, when searching online for something, will give up after going a few pages into the search engine results pages. In some cases, a search may produce millions of hits. Needless to say, you do not want to go through every one in order to find what you are looking for. Most people have neither the time or the inclination to do this.

This is why it is so important for businesses and others who want to have their website noticed make sure that they use SEO techniques in order to do so. By using SEO, a website will no longer be buried in the middle or at the end of millions of results. It has a better chance of getting to the front of the search engine results pages.

SEO has several close relatives. **SEM**, or **search engine marketing**, is a broader term that refers to SEO as well as paid search placement, contextual advertising, and paid inclusion advertising. It is also important to think of SEO as including *conversion optimization*—the study and practice of improving the conversion of visitors to customers after they visit your web page.

Always consider that a search engine's core purpose is to deliver relevant search results to a user entering a query.

Older readers will recall using the Lycos search engine at one time, but almost no one uses the service any more. Why not? Because the Lycos search engine didn't return very good results for users. Either the results were not relevant, or the results were diluted with ads. For whatever reason, Lycos was not as good as Google at delivering a relevant set of usable results in response to a query.

It's important to keep in mind the role of the search engine. Too often, webmasters think or say Google is *against* them because Google appears to rank lower-value sites in favor of their own. The truth is the exact opposite: Google wants you to rank—as long as your result serves the needs of its user base. You need to give Google what it's looking for (or Yahoo or Bing, as the case may be), and Google will rank your site higher.

While Google is the leading search engine in the Western Hemisphere, there are, of course, alternative search engines such as Yandex in Russia and Baidu in China. The fortunes of the various search engines ebb and flow, with Google maintaining a commanding lead. Comscore.com is a well-regarded analyst of search engine metrics and reports that in 2014, Google's share of US search queries at about 75 percent, Yahoo at about 10 percent, and Bing/Microsoft at about 10 percent. The remaining field is made up of a handful of 3rd-tier search engines like Ask.com (http://www.ask.com/), Blekko.com (http://blekko.com/), and hundreds of smaller search engines.

So, how does one rank for all search engines? The answer is easy: optimize for Google. Google's search algorithm is the most advanced, and is certainly the best at detecting disfavored optimization techniques such as keywords stuffing, paid link arrangements, and the like. Furthermore, Google's technology is so dominant that the other search engines imitate most of Google's innovations.

And so, if you rank well for Google, you'll certainly be well-positioned to rank well in the other search engines. Keep in mind, however, that Google is also the most responsive search engine. Google crawls (visits) your site more often, and indexes websites faster than the other search engines. So, as you work on optimization, you might see positive changes in Google rankings in a few weeks, whereas the other search engines might take months to respond.

# CHAPTER 2 - How SEARCH ENGINE works?

Keep an open mind about what constitutes a search engine. The traditional definition of a search engine—a destination website into which desktop-based users enter typed search queries is already eroding. For several years, Google has been testing, tweaking, and improving its voice recognition system. It was clear early on that Google had already envisioned a day in the near future where search queries would be voiced rather than typed. Sure enough, the increasingly popular Android mobile device platform has voice recognition technology integrated into its architecture.

The near future will bring further progress in the types of devices on which users perform searches as well as the input device into which these searches are made. Near term trending shows that we'll see growth in both mobile-based searches and voice-input searches. Staying ahead of trends in search can help you best your competitors in search rankings.

While the type of input device doesn't necessarily change the fundamental nature of search, the increasing variety of specialized search properties does. In recent years, an increasing number of specialized sites have emerged for special-purpose searches. Yelp.com is a destination site for people seeking highly recommended local businesses and hot spots.

Dedicated apps like Restaurant Finder on popular mobile platforms help users find restaurants near their current location. Goby is a recent search engine specifically designed to help users find activities in a local area. This is a trend—the first search engines were either directories, single search boxes, or both. Now, there are thousands of individual properties employing hundreds of different approaches to search.

One of my favorite academic questions to ask people about search technology is, *when do you think internet searching was invented?* While the exact date is elusive, the answer is nearly always wrong—by several decades. Routinely, people reflect the common understanding that search technology was invented in the 1990s.

Actually, a search engine merely employs search query and indexing principles that were conceived and implemented decades before in a mainframe environment. Indexing, coupled with search queries, allowed early computer operators to quickly select relevant information from large databases in the infancy of the computer age. The Internet is simply a much larger database and a modern search engine is simply a much more robust and sophisticated search query tool.

A search engine does not store your web pages; it stores an index of your web pages. For your page to appear in a search engine's index, first that search engine sends a search spider to visit your site and read your web pages' content. The spider returns the information to a document processor that processes your web pages into a format that the query processor understands.

The document processor performs several formatting tasks—it might remove stop words, lower-value terms that bear little relation to the page's topic, such as *the*, *and*, *it*, and many more. The document processor will also perform term stemming, where suffixes like *-ing*, *-er*, *-es*, and *-ed* are stripped from search terms. In essence, a document processor trims the content to reveal the contextual elements of a web page and prepares the entry for indexing.

The index contains much of the information from your pages, along with other data that the search engine uses to evaluate and categorize your pages. As a highly simplified example, Google's index of your page will contain the text of your page on a date in the recent past when its spider last visited along with other data which are as follows:

- A table of terms in order of the frequency in which they appear on your page (called the inverted file)
- The page's PageRank
- A term weight assignment: a numerical value that reflects the frequency of appearance of particular terms on a page
- The page's meta tags
- The page's destination URL

Once the index is prepared, the page is available for querying. The query processor, along with a search and matching engine, performs the nuts and bolts of the search function—matching a user's query to stored entries in the search engine's index. The final element is a sound methodology for ranking the query results. If all works as planned, the search engine returns a sensibly ordered set of results to each user's query.

Peeking into the mechanics of search gives us a few guidelines to follow. One core principle that emerges is this—words are the food upon which search engines feed. Without relevant, contextual words on your pages, the search engines cannot accurately index your pages. The other important idea is that a search engine searches an index—it doesn't search your pages directly. So, if your pages aren't in the index, they aren't going to be found. These concepts will re-emerge as we work through the chapters in this book.

# CHAPTER 3 – UNDERSTANDING THE FULL ON PAGE SEARCH ENGINE RANKING FACTOR.

SEO professionals lump search engine optimization techniques and thought into three categories—on-page optimization, off-page optimization, and conversion. On-page optimization is concerned with all of the text, images, code, words, navigation, structure, and so on that appear on your website—all of the factors you control that appear *on-page*. Off-page optimization refers to all of the material on the Internet concerning or pointing to your website that does not appear *on-page*; for the most part, off-page optimization refers to inbound links on third-party websites. Conversion refers to how effective your website is at making users take actions, once they appear on your site. A high-performing website needs all three elements working together.

On-page factors include the following:

- The body content—the main text of the page
- Title and meta tags
- Heading tags (h1, h2, h3)
- The quality and complexity of the HTML and CSS code that generates the webpage
- The images, their filenames and alt tags
- Text attributes such as the use of bold and underline
- Outbound links—their number and the anchor text used in each
- The use of either do follow or no follow attributes on any of the links

- The internal navigation and link structure
- The size of your files and the speed at which your website loads
- The total number of pages on your website
- The rate at which you update or add content to your website

But how important are each of these factors? How do we know that one factor is more important than another? The software or programs that Google and the other search engines use to determine rankings are referred to as an *algorithm*. While the behavior of search engines can sometimes appear remarkably intuitive and almost human, the science underlying a search algorithm is url Not all on-page elements are as important as others—search engines must assign particular importance or weight to various on-page factors. A webpage's title tag, for example, is widely considered to be a strong indicator of the subject matter of a webpage. As such, a title tag has a very strong influence on search rankings.

Conversely, the filenames of the images on a webpage, such as `texas_web_ marketing.jpg`, would not necessarily be a strong indicator of the subject matter of a webpage. So, search engines apply much less weight to image file names in their ranking algorithms. The basket of on-page factors that influence search engine rankings are afforded a wide variation in influence in search engine rankings—this variance is referred to by SEO professionals as *weight*.

Title tags and heading tags are afforded greater weight, while image filenames, alt tags (text tags that accompany images), and bold text are given less weight. That is not to say that bold text and image filenames are not important. In fact, it's the use of these lower-weight attributes that can give a webpage the extra push to higher rankings. When all of the ranking factors are present and utilized effectively and combined with a sound program of developing inbound links, the effect is almost supernatural—the combined effect of all factors working together can develop tremendous ranking power.

## Body Content

Body content simply means the *words on the page*, actual ASCII text readable by a search engine. This important factor is too often ignored by webmasters. Some of the most egregious examples of webmasters that miss this important factor are sites with little or no text, sites that rely on image files to display text and messages, and flash-based sites. Search engines do not read the text in pictures or effectively read the text in flash files. So, if you are describing your service in an image file, JavaScript, or a flash file, your message will not be read, and you will not rank for those terms.

A search engine needs to be able to find text on a webpage in order to make an evaluation of what your page is about. The text on your pages should meet the following rules:

- **Size**: A webpage should have at least 250 words of readable ASCII text
- **Focus**: A webpage should be focused on a reasonably narrow set of keywords
- **Keyword Density**: A webpage should not have keywords repeated, so that the density of the keywords is too high in relation to the total number of words

A webpage should be of a reasonable length, at least 250 words. A page length of 400 or 500 words is better, but one can get by with shorter pages in some cases. In a more competitive search market, 250 words may not be enough and you'll need to increase your page length to rank effectively.

A webpage's body text should be focused—the page should speak to a narrow set of keyword phrases and not try to cover too much ground. If your webpages cover too many separate topics or keyword phrases in one page, you'll dilute the ranking power of each individual phrase and you'll rank for nothing.

You need to stay on-topic. If you are creating a page describing your expert IT services, don't fill the page up with 60 percent testimonials; those testimonials may have value to your readers—and testimonials certainly have a place and a role in creating websites where your target readers are potential customers—but testimonials will not necessarily contain the keywords for which you want to rank. So, keep your webpages' body text focused on the topic of that page.

Similarly, don't cover too many topics within your body text. For example, say you want to create an Amazon affiliate page on your website and try to rank for *WordPress books*, *Joomla books*, and *books on web design*. If you try to rank for all three keywords on one page, you'll have to divide your content among a discussion of these separate topics. You'll dilute your ranking power for the phrase *WordPress books* by repeating the terms *Joomla books* and *books on web design* within the body text of your page. The better approach is to build three separate pages, each with a focus on one related family of keywords. Conversely, if you wanted to rank for *WordPress books, books on WordPress,* and *best WordPress books,* you could create a single page to rank for all those terms because you can easily write body text which includes all those phrases. Your focused page will rank quite well.

## Title & Meta Tag

Title tags and meta tags are strings of text that are inserted in the head section of a webpage. These tags are inconspicuous to a user, although not entirely hidden. The title tag appears in the top bar of the user's browser window, but does not appear on the webpage itself. The meta tags do not appear to the user, they are intended for search engines to read. The principal meta tags for use in search optimization are meta keyword tags and meta description tags.

Title tags are the most important ranking factor on an individual webpage; they are highly weighted by the search engines.

Often, a simple change to a title tag alone can yield significant changes in rankings. Again, remember the role of a search engine to determine the topic of a webpage and return relevant results to its users. The title tag, logically, is perhaps the greatest signpost of what a page is actually about.

Title tags serve another important role, when a user enters a search query into a search engine, the first line of each entry on a search engine results pages are taken from each page's title tag. So, now your title tag presents an opportunity to attract searchers to click on your result out of a field of other websites on a search engine results page. Not only that, both Yahoo and Google bold the words used in the search query within the title tags that they display on the search engine results page. So, if you use keywords effectively in your title tag, Google will highlight your entry in the search engine results page and that can help increase the click-through rate to your website pages.

## Proper Use of The Heading

The earliest specifications for HTML included provisions for document headings and subheadings, elements known as heading tags. Heading tag elements begin at `h1` and progress to `h6`, each level is intended to represent an ordered and organized taxonomy. These tags serve multiple roles.

As mark-up tags, these elements conveniently format the text elements to which they are applied. For example, an `h1` tag will generate large text, in a bold font, with margins above and below—much like the headline in a newspaper article.

As HTML standards matured and CSS formatting became available in browsers, many web designers abandoned heading tags in search of prettier formatting for their headings. True, you can make text big and bold with CSS mark-up or with HTML formatting; you can make any text look like a heading without utilizing heading tags. However, in the world of search that is a blunder because you will build almost no search engine ranking power from simply formatting text.

For search engines, heading tags serve a supplemental function beyond formatting. Heading tags serve as signposts, that help search engines determine the context and topic of a web page. Heading tags are certainly part of search algorithms, and are given moderate weight in determining search position.

The best methodology for employing heading tags is to do the following. First, your page should only employ an `h1` tag once. The text of the `h1` tag should describe the main topic of the web page upon which it appears and should include the high-value, high-volume keywords for which you want to rank. Next, at a minimum you should employ both `h1` and `h2` tags. Your `h2` tags should repeat your important keywords—but with additional terms to give context to the section that the `h2` tag covers. For example, if you are writing a page about air conditioning service and repair, you might employ `h2` tags with text such as, *Your best choice for air conditioning service*, and *Licensed and insured air conditioning service*.

The `h3` tags are optional, but can come in handy for organizing longer pages. The search engine ranking power of heading tags decreases as you progress from `h1` down through the lower orders of heading tags. Thus, `h1` tags are mandatory, `h2` tags are highly recommended, and `h3` tags are necessary only in the most competitive markets. Heading tags have a complementary effect when combined with an effective title tag, body text, and meta description—when these elements are in accord, a search engine can more comfortably determine the main context of a web page, and can more confidently reward that web page with higher rankings.

Remember also, that keyword prominence applies to heading tags, so greater weight is given to the words at the beginning of the tag.

# Page Loading Time/Page Loading Speed

Code quality is an often overlooked element of search ranking. Because it's overlooked, it represents a great opportunity to edge out less alert or less informed competitors. Code quality refers to the quality, amount, and load speed of the code and image sizes underline your website. Search engines like quality code and fast loading times; poor quality code and slow loading times mean a poor user experience for searchers.

HTML is an open source family of mark-up languages designed with fairly strict specifications set forth by the **World Wide Web Consortium (W3C)**. These standards are updated every few years and result in new versions of HTML, such as the upgrade from HTML 4 to HTML 5.

When the code quality underlying a website does not meet the specifications of the HTML standard, the website may not display properly in all browsers. If the code is filled with errors or lacks proper elements such as an HTML doctype declaration, then that website may actually perform poorly in search engines. To test your code for validation, visit the W3C's free validator at `https://validator.w3.org/`.

The amount of code underlying the website can affect its load speed. The proper use of CSS can help a website reduce mindless repetition of attribute statements like font-size and color. Users of WordPress can worry less about code quality. Assuming that the WordPress template employed by a website does not contain coding errors, WordPress generally delivers very lean code that validates perfectly. You can test your website's CSS code by using W3C's free CSS validator at `https://jigsaw.w3.org/css-validator/`.

Image size can also affect load speed. Always be sure you are using a compressed image format whenever possible. For example, use the JPEG format for photographs with an appropriate amount of compression. The faster the images load, the faster your webpages will load.

## Internal Link Structure

Link architecture refers to the way a website's menus and navigation links are constructed. Link architecture can be very powerful and it's also one of the hardest topics in search to truly master.

The anchor text (the blue underlined text) of a website link is a ranking factor whether that link is from a site linking into your site, or is simply a link on your own site leading to another page within your site. For that reason, you have an opportunity to rank for certain terms by carefully selecting the anchor text that you use in your navigation menus. The most perfect example of the misuse of this principle in practice is the common employment of the term *Home* as the anchor text in navigation menus to point to a website's home page. A website's homepage has more ranking potential than any interior page on a website. For that reason, the anchor text pointing to the home page should be carefully selected. For example, instead of *Home*, consider employing keyword-rich phrases such as *Austin's Best Carpet Cleaning* or *VW Repair* as the navigation anchor text.

Another common mistake in site architecture and site structure is the use of image buttons for links. A link comprised solely of an image has no anchor text. It's a missed opportunity to include a keyword in a text link and send a signal to the search engines about what the topic of the destination page is. It's curious to see that this practice is still employed so often.

Other issues arise in link architecture when the navigation menus are written in JavaScript or Flash—search engines don't read those languages effectively. The safest approach to constructing navigation menus is with HTML. If you require active navigation—dropdown or flyout sub-menus—make sure they are constructed with search-friendly code such as CSS. Or, the problem of *shifting navigation*, where the navigation menus change as the user moves through a site. A good rule to follow is that if navigation is confusing for users, it's probably confusing for search engine spiders as well.

When securing inbound links from other websites, you would never want high number/high proportion links that all use the exact anchor text—you'll likely trip a search engine filter if you do. Google wants to see natural linking patterns. A website with hundreds of links that all have the same anchor text (that is, *New York Dentist*) does not look natural to a search engine, so a ranking filter would likely be imposed by the search engine to knock that listing down a few pages. The anchor text you choose for your site-wide navigation serves as an opportunity to use anchor text in higher numbers and in higher proportion that you wouldn't use for external links. The search engines have no anchor text penalty for your internal links, you can point 100 percent of your internal links to your front page with any anchor text you like.

Finally, the great opportunity with link architecture is simply to make sure the number and quality of links are pointing in greater numbers to the high-value pages such as your home page and product pages, and are pointing in lower numbers to your low value pages such as your privacy policy, your contact form, and your return policy. An easy way to accomplish this, is to simply have your standard navigation either horizontally at the top of your website, or on a left or right sidebar; then, to send extra link power to your most important pages, create a footer with links to your home page and a few other high-value pages. Additionally, you can always create extra link power by creating text links to your key pages within the body of text throughout your site.

WordPress handles link architecture well. WordPress presents very simple site-wide navigation menus by default. In fact, many have criticized WordPress for not offering users as much control over navigation menus as they would like. With WordPress releases beginning with 3.0, however, WordPress users enjoy the ability to customize navigation menus with the new menu feature, available under the appearance tab in the WordPress dashboard.

For users less experienced with SEO, we recommend sticking with WordPress' reliable default navigation.

The customizable navigation is flexible and powerful—but that flexibility and power in inexperienced hands can yield poor search ranking results.

## Image Optimization

Image names and image alt tags are an example of a ranking factor that is afforded lower weight in search rankings, that is, `wordpress-expert.jpg` as a filename in an attempt to rank for *WordPress expert*. Certainly, image names alone will never make anyone rank for any term or phrase that is highly competitive. However, image names and alt tags can be effective as supplemental weight for search terms when the more important elements such as title tags and heading tags are highly focused and in accord.

## Fresh Content

Search engines respond to fresh, original content. Even more, search engines love a steady stream of fresh, original content.

I am sure we have all heard people talk about the website they are about to launch, saying *I am having a website built and it is almost finished*. When I hear that exact phrase—and I hear it a lot—I cringe just a bit and feel like responding, *Really? Well, my website will never be finished*. That's because a website should be alive and constantly changing. The old way of thinking about websites is that when a website was finished, it would sit frozen and immovable until the next redesign. Even the word *site* implies something fixed in the ground, not something constantly in motion.

A search engine sees a website for what it is. If a website has static content that never changes, the search engine knows it. Over time, the search engine spiders will come less often. Why send a search spider for content that doesn't change? The site will not be seen by search engines as high-value to its users. On the other hand, publish regular content to your site and the search engines will know it. In fact, search engines are moving toward real-time search results, although this technology isn't yet fully developed. The search engines will send spiders to your site more often looking for both new content and changes to old content. Your site will rise in the rankings. And, if that wasn't enough, new content will get a fresh content bump.

The fresh content bump refers to a supplemental boost in ranking power that search engines assign to fresh content served up from blogging platforms like WordPress for the first few weeks after the published date.

WordPress began as a pure blogging platform and the search engines see new WordPress posts as timely, topical, and potentially newsworthy items. The search engines reward new posts with a little boost in position. As time passes, the posts will settle down in the rankings. You can use the fresh content bump to cleverly schedule prime rankings for matters of seasonal interest to readers. For example, you would write a post titled "Spring Activities in South Florida, 2016" where you deftly advertise your scuba diving service along with other activities. If you time it right, you'll get a boost in rankings right when the last tourists are having their vacations.

Your fresh content need not be entirely free give-aways with no benefit to you. Your new content can be a post or page about how you now serve a new area; put the name of the new town in the page as a keyword, and you'll rank for searches in which that town name appears. Or, how about a page announcing a summer sale? Google likes new content—but it doesn't have to be completely fantastic content every time.

Another benefit: new content is great when it is new, but new content is also pretty great when it is old. A site with continually fresh content becomes a very large site very quickly. We discussed the benefits of a large site in the previous section.

If you are reading this book, you likely have a WordPress site or are considering a WordPress site. With WordPress, your ease and speed of publishing is unmatched— you'll create new and better content faster than other webmasters, your site will be alive with regularly fresh content and your site will grow up quickly.

# CHAPTER 4 – UNDERSTANDING THE FULL OFF PAGE SEARCH ENGINE RANKING FACTOR.

You can also gain ranking power by making outbound links from your site to other sites. The theory goes something like the following. You have a website for your gardening business and you want to rank for the phrase "gardening service San Diego." If you have an outbound link to other sites about gardening services and the anchor text of that outbound link is "gardening service", then that link can serve as a signpost to search engines that your site is about gardening services.

This technique has a potential disadvantage (there's disagreement within the SEO community about this point that remains unresolved): by linking to other sites, you are directing valuable PageRank away from your page to the page to which you are linking. So, you lose some PageRank, but gain ranking power for the keyword. You may not want to overdo it—maybe just a few outbound links on a few pages, and always to reputable websites. This is a technique that requires some finesse, so you might employ some testing to see where outbound linking can be most effective.

Off-page ranking factors can be summarized with one phrase: inbound links. Inbound links from other websites are the real power that makes sites rank. In the competitive search markets, links might comprise 80 to 90 percent of the work that goes into a website.

The best way to think of the relationship between on-page factors an off-page factors is this: on-page factors are like tuning up a car for a race to make sure all the parts run reliably and strongly, off-page factors are the fuel.

So, if your car isn't running right, all the fuel in the world isn't going to make it go. Similarly, if you don't have any fuel, even the most highly-tuned car will go nowhere. In the world of search optimization, you need both.

Google, more than any other search engine, was the great innovator with respect to measuring inbound linking power and then adjusting search results in favor of sites that enjoy high numbers of inbound links. The reasoning is sound: sites with high numbers of inbound links are most likely superior websites, to those that have low numbers of inbound links. This innovation that links between websites are *votes* for the quality of the destination site, is now employed by all major search engines. And, for the most part, the principle does ensure superior search results when users search for information through a search engine.

What Google wants, ideally, is for inbound links to be natural links, not artificially generated links. If a website owner earns inbound links through paid link-building schemes, then the methodology is skewed—the lower value site that has paid for inbound links now enjoys higher ranking power than a superior site with fewer links. That result is not what is intended by the inbound link component of the search algorithms.

The search engines know that in the real world, not all linking between websites will be natural. They are fully aware that webmasters attempt to game the system through a variety of linking practices that range from relatively innocent reciprocal linking to more sinister practices, like automated forum spamming and hidden links. Google forbids *link schemes* in its webmaster guidelines, and penalties are common.

The task for the legitimate webmaster is to secure links naturally. Natural linking will ensure that your site will never suffer a penalty, and links that you obtain naturally will carry much more power than links obtained through any schemes or artificial means. We cover specific line building methods in *Chapter 6, Link Building*.

## Careful About Over-Optimization

Over-optimization occurs when a website's elements are present in too high a proportion or too high in power for a given keyword phrase. Over-optimization yields poor search performance. An example of over-optimization would be the incessant use of keywords on your website, so that your keywords represent 50 percent of the total density of words on the page. Another example would be a website with 100 inbound links, all with the same exact anchor text. First-time SEO hobbyists tend to be ensnared by over-optimization as they zealously pursue the new elements of SEO that they learn; they stuff keywords into title tags, meta tags, body text, and secure links all with the same anchor text.

Over-optimization is difficult to quantify, and can be difficult to detect and repair. The best way to think about over-optimization is that websites should never be *too perfect*. Remember, a search engine ultimately must employ mathematics to its ranking criteria. It's easy for a search engine to mathematically determine that a page with a keyword density—keywords as a percentage of total words on the page—exceeding 8 percent is attempting to game the algorithm and therefore should not be ranked.

Thinking about over-optimization in this way, repetition is often the main culprit. To avoid over-optimization you'll need to be vigilant to watch for excessive repetition of terms in the main elements of a website and in inbound links. In other words, just do good writing and the rest will follow naturally. You wouldn't keep repeating yourself in good writing.

## Conversion is Important

Too often, people think of SEO solely in terms of ranking position. They forget that if your website cannot turn that casual visitor into a customer—your ranking did nothing for you except send a visitor to your site for a moment.

Conversion science is the discipline of making sure the visitors to your site take some action to bring them closer to being a customer. Successful websites have specific and effective calls to action. A call to action is a phrase, graphic, or a section of your website that urges the visitor to take some tangible step toward becoming a customer or user of your product or website. The call to action can be a box that says *Call Now for Immediate Service*, *Shop Now!*, or *Subscribe for Free! Get Updates by RSS*.

A call to action doesn't necessarily mean that visitors purchase something right there, but that they take steps toward becoming a purchaser.

Your call to action will differ based on the space in which you compete. If you are a blogger and want to expand the reach of your blog, you'll want users to sign up to your RSS feed, or follow you on Twitter. In more traditional business environments, like retail and home services, you'll want people to call or e-mail to make an appointment. In a full e-commerce environment, you'll want to immediately drive people to make purchases.

For your calls to action to be effective, you need to keep them prominent, above the fold (on the upper part of your web pages that are visible before scrolling down is required), and persuasive. *Above the fold* is a term from the newspaper industry, meaning above the halfway point where a newspaper was folded.

Another rule of conversions is to have fallback positions, a second best option. In other words, if your users don't purchase something today maybe they'll sign up for your Twitter feed, which lets you keep them updated to new products. Perhaps later, these new contacts will eventually become customers.

## Creating Conversion Based Website Boost Ranking

Each competitive space is different. However, conversion science does teach a few absolute principles that can help you create highly effective conversion-based websites:

- Don't hide contact information. About 30 percent of all websites do not display contact information prominently. In a business environment, this mistake is pure suicide. Put that phone number and e-mail up top where users can find it.

- Put the meat where the eyes are. Use the "above the fold" portions your header and sidebars for conversion tools and messages. Studies show that user's eyes typically scan the top and sidebar areas for information. Don't expect users to scroll to hunt for your phone number.
- Mix it up. Some users like to call, others like to e-mail. Give users more than one choice.
- Don't frustrate your users by directing them to non-functioning elements. For example, don't use *Chat now* buttons that lead to dead ends, that is, *Chat is not available right now*. If you utilize a call to action, make absolutely sure the action is available, even if it's a voice mail, that is still better than wasting a customer's time.
- Don't broadcast your poor service. Don't say *To reach sales, call between 1pm and 5pm*. That's just begging your customers to go elsewhere. If you must be out of the office (all of us must leave work sometimes) just send folks to a friendly voicemail and return the call later.
- Give fewer choices. Don't confuse readers with too many selections. If your viewers get confused or overwhelmed, they might slip into *choice paralysis*.
- Always give the next step. Don't lose your customers along the way. If they don't buy, get them to sign up for your newsletter. If you convert them to watch your video, make the next step an invitation to purchase.
- Sell benefits, not features. *Your car will run faster!* will convert better than *Our fuel additives are the most powerful in the industry.*
- Use testimonials. Tell your customers what other users say about your service.

- Guide their eyes and attention. You can literally point users to your desired action with arrows and buttons.

The following screenshot of Google's Cloud Print service shows several elements of expert conversion science at work. The user is guided visually to the call to action with a clear and simple button in a contrasting color. The benefit, *Print anywhere, from any device*, is short and clear. The page is uncluttered, which enables a clearer path to action for the user. The placement of the conversion tool is above the fold: Truly effective calls to action are going to differ widely depending on the space in which you participate. You'll want to try different approaches and measure your results. In *Chapter 10, Testing Your Site and Monitoring Your Progress*, we'll cover how to measure the performance of your website.

# CHAPTER 5 – INTRODUCING CLICKBANK & SELECTING OUR PRODUCT.

We are going to select Right away an affiliate product that we are going to promote to earn affiliate commission. If you are newbie to SEO and Affiliate Marketing, I would recommend to start with Clickbank Affiliate Network.

There are a lot of other Affiliate Networks including and you can find more about them <u>here</u>. Right now however, we are going to pick a product from Clickbank Affiliate Network.

Visit Clickbank: <u>http://www.clickbank.com/</u>. You can Join through the SignUp Link as per below picture

Now you need to fill your information on the next page.

After providing all information and completing the whole process, you will be provided a nickname which is your Affiliate ID.

Once you have an Id from Clickbank. You can promote any products you like. You can ask me the question? Why I choose Clickbank rather than any other affiliate marketplace? Because Clickbank has the best ever products what is very easy to sell and they have a huge collection. Apart from that you can get your commission instantly when you make a sell. Also, we can promote any products you like without asking for the permission. The commission is also very high 40%-75%, sometimes even more.

There is a lots of well-known marketplace where you have to wait for days to get the approval of promoting a product. Sometimes the vendor or products owner also decline the newbie and it is really tough and annoying for getting started on those platforms.

So, if you are just starting your journey in online platform then Clickbank will be the best choice for you.

Don't worry guys!! who have previous experience in online platform or who doesn't want to start with Clickbank we will talk about the other affiliate networks later section in this book. I will personally recommend Clickbank as it has worked for me so well. But you can choose any other affiliate network as you like.

Anyway you got your affiliate Id, congratulations!!!! Now you can promote any products from the Clickbank marketplace.

Here is a picture of Clickbank Marketplace,

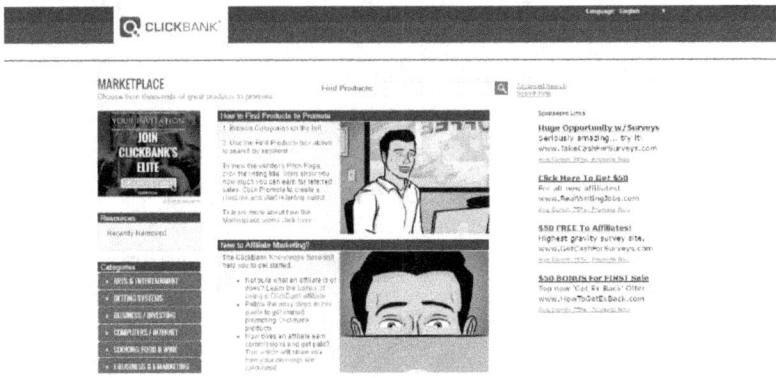

All products from all niches are listed here by Clickbank Vendors. You are now going to pick one product from the categories. Normally these categories are also known as a Niche. So you will select your niche first and then find a hot product in it. Being an experienced Affiliate Marketer, I recommend you to select from any of these products I will mention bellow.

1. Green Products.
2. Health & Fitness.

3. Home & Garden.
4. Software & Services.

You might be thinking!!!!?? Those 4 category is so competitive if you are familiar with these one. It is true that those are very competitive but I have believed in my "SEO+Clickbank" book and my books ranking power. I strongly believe that if you follow my step by step process then you can generate sells by using the SEO strategy we will discuss later in this book.

Still if you ask about my personal choice, I normally choose Health & Fitness as I am in the weight loss niche, so most of the products I promote fall under Health & Fitness niche. Also, don't worry about niche competitiveness, the ranking system I am going to lay down for you in coming chapters is so much powerful that you can rank your site in any niche even it is not an affiliate sitemagical ranking shifts for every keyword you select for ranking.

There are 3 factors I always look for when selecting a product for promoting.

1. Popularity.
2. Gravity.
3. Commission Per Sale.

Thinking about these 3 very important things and by a good research I select this winning products for my affiliate earning.

Now you need to generate your hop link or Affiliate Link which you need to send potential buyers to "The Venus Factor" product sales page. Once somebody will buy this product through your hop link, you will get commission on that sale.

Let's generate one,

Click on Promote and on the next page you need to put your affiliate id (your account nickname) to get your Clickbank hop link (or Affiliate Link).

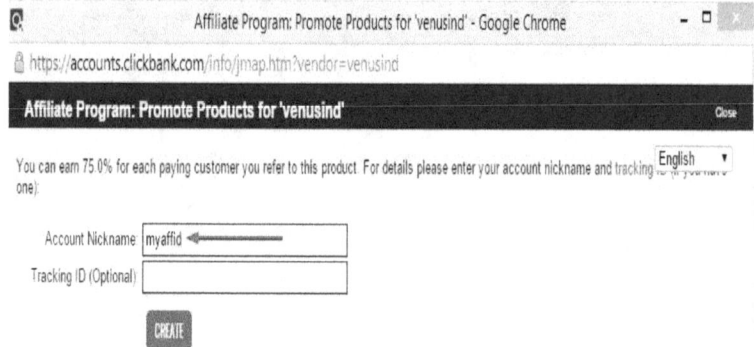

I just put a fake name but you have to put your real affiliate name and hit the create button. That's it you generated your hoplink.

Be careful of putting your real affiliate id, as without putting the real code or nickname you can't get any money when you sell a product. So be sure to double check it.

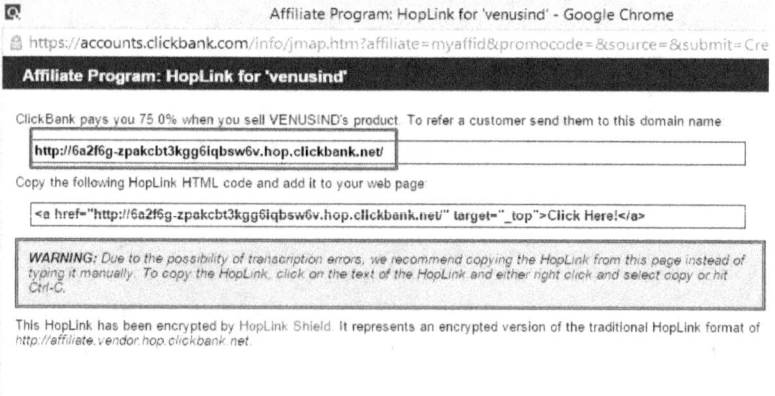

# CHAPTER 6 – BRAINSTORMING THE KEYWORDS.

I was talking with a client some time ago who wanted to have his site rank well in the search engines. The client is a company with annual revenues in the millions of dollars, in the business of, oh, I don't know . . . Staging rodent-racing events. (I've changed the details of this story a tad to protect the guilty.)

I did a little research and found that most people searching for rodent-racing events use the keywords rodent racing. (Big surprise, huh?) I took a look at the client's Web site and discovered that the words rodent racing didn't appear anywhere on the site's Web pages.

"You have a little problem," I said. "Your site doesn't use the words rodent racing, so it's unlikely that any search engine will find your site when people search for that." "Oh, well," was the client's reply, "our marketing department objects to the term. We have a company policy to use the term furry friend events.

The term rodent is too demeaning, and if we say we're racing them, the animal rights people will get upset." This is a real story; well, except for the bit about rodent racing and the furry friend's thing. But, in principle, it happened. This company had a policy not to use the words that most of its potential clients were using to search for it.

This is an unusual example, in which a company knows the important keywords but decides not to use them. But, in fact, many companies build Web sites only to discover later that the keywords its potential clients and visitors are using are not on the site. How is that possible? Well, I can think of a couple of reasons:

✓ Most sites are built without any regard for search engines. The site designers simply don't think about search engines or have little background knowledge of how search engines work.

✓ The site designers do think about search engines, but they guess, often incorrectly, what keywords they should be using. I can't tell you how the client and I resolved his problem because, well, we didn't. (Sometimes company politics trump common sense.) But in this chapter, I explain how to pick keywords that make sense for your site, as well as how to discover what keywords your potential site visitors are using to search for your products and services.

When you use a search engine, you type in a word or words and click the Search button. The search engine then looks in its index for those words. Suppose that you typed rodent racing. Generally speaking, the search engine looks for

- ✓ Pages that contain the exact phrase rodent racin

- ✓ Pages that don't have the phrase rodent racing but do have the words rodent and racing in close proximity

- ✓ Pages that have the words rodent and racing somewhere, though not necessarily close together

- ✓ Pages with word stems; for instance, pages with the word rodent and the word race somewhere in the page

- ✓ Pages with synonyms, such as, perhaps, mouse and rat

- ✓ Pages that have links pointing to them, in which the link text contains the phrase rodent racing

- ✓ Pages with links pointing to them with the link text containing the words rodent and racing, although not together.

The process is actually a lot more complicated. The search engine doesn't necessarily show pages in the order I just listed — all the pages with the exact phrase, and then all the pages with the words in close proximity, and so on. When considering ranking order, the search engine considers (in addition to hundreds of secret criteria) whether the keyword or phrase is in

- ✓ Bold text

- ✓ Italicized text

✓ Bulleted lists

✓ Text larger than other text on the page

✓ Heading text (<H> tags)

Despite the various complications, however, one fact is of paramount importance: If a search engine can't relate your Web site to the words that someone searches for, it has no reason to return your Web site as part of the search results.

Picking the right keywords is critical. As Woody Allen once said, "Eighty percent of success is showing up." If you don't play the game, you can't win. And if you don't choose the right keywords, you're not even showing up to play the game. If a specific keyword or keyword phrase doesn't appear in your pages (or in links pointing to your pages), your site will not appear when someone enters those keywords into the search engines. For instance, say you're a technical writer in San Diego, and you have a site with the term technical writer scattered throughout. You will not appear in search results when someone searches for technical writer san diego if you don't have the words San Diego in your pages. Understanding how to search helps you understand the role of keywords.

You can use some of the keyword researching tools for further assistance,

1. Google Keyword Planner Tool
2. Word tracker
3. Bing Keyword Planner Tool
4. Semrush.com.

# CHAPTER 7 – FORECAST FUTURE EARNING.

Some people might think this is unnecessary. But the reality is if you know the results we will earn upfront then you will be determining enough to succeed.

In SEO & Affiliate Marketing you have to be self-determined. Hard work and regular activity is very important and when you want some quick success then you have to give double effort for gaining the result. In this chapter we will forecast your future earning, if you follow "SEO+ClickBank" step by step then you will gain quick success in no time. Also, you can earn this amount of money daily, what I will discuss next.

So, without wasting any more time. Let's get have a look at our future earning.

Now it is the time to analyze that whether keywords that I have selected are great or not with respect to affiliate commission once site is ranked.

Frankly, you can't predict how much affiliate commission you will earn from an affiliate site in the initial phase. But determining in advance (even a rough idea) will surely motivate you to work on your project.

I actually used a commission forecasting Excel Sheet (not 100% Correct) for predicting commission if I hit position one.

Fat Loss Factor Commission Forecasting. These Stats were pre forecasted before I started setting up my affiliate site. This commission forecast was based on the assumption that our site will rank at position one.

| Keyword | Search Volume | Percentage | Site Traffic | Conversion Rate | Monthly Income | Daily Income |
|---|---|---|---|---|---|---|
| fat loss factor | 12,100 | 0.5 | 6050 | 0.6% | $1,325 | $91 |
| fat loss factor review | 2,900 | 0.5 | 1450 | 0.6% | $365.40 | $12 |
| fat loss factor program | 1,600 | 0.5 | 800 | 0.6% | $202 | $7 |
| fat loss factor reviews | 1,300 | 0.5 | 650 | 0.6% | $164 | $5 |
| the fat loss factor | 880 | 0.5 | 440 | 0.6% | $111 | $4 |
| fat loss factor scam | 880 | 0.5 | 440 | 0.6% | $111 | $4 |
| fat loss factor free | 590 | 0.5 | 295 | 0.6% | $74 | $2 |
| fat loss factor program review | 390 | 0.5 | 195 | 0.6% | $49 | $2 |
| fat loss factor book | 390 | 0.5 | 195 | 0.6% | $49 | $2 |
| fat loss factor diet | 260 | 0.5 | 130 | 0.6% | $33 | $1 |

| | |
|---|---|
| Conversion Rate (Money Site) | 20% |
| Conversion Rate (Product Page) | 3% |
| Commission Per Sale (CPC) | $42 |
| Total Monthly Income | $2,683 |
| Total Daily Income | $89 |

Just fill all pointed field and you will have commission forecasting for your keywords when those keywords ranked for Position #1.

Most of required data to fill the commission forecasting sheet will be available at the time of product selection through Clickbank marketplace. Just grab those numbers and put into this sheet to have some idea in advance how much you will earn later on.

Truly Speaking, A decent commission forecasting always motivates me personally to work more and put extra effort to achieve desired results. However, as of today, I am on page one and my positions are normally stable between 1 to 5 for most of the keyword but still making more than this commission forecasting. I am on average making 100$ a day from this site.

You can check ranking stats in Module 0 where I have described about My Case Study. Go and check live ranking stats there.

Always try to hit Page 1 first and then put more effort to rank your keywords for the page.

# CHAPTER 8 – PICKING & SET UP DOMAIN+HOSTING

## Hosting

Although many large companies place their Web sites on their own Web servers, most small companies don't. They shouldn't do this, in fact, because there's simply no way you can do it anywhere near as cheaply and reliably as a good hosting company can do it. Rather, a hosting company rents space on its servers to other businesses. Although you have to consider many factors when selecting a hosting company, I focus on the factors related to search engine optimization.

When looking for a hosting company, make sure that you can

✓ Upload Web pages you created by yourself. Some services provide simple tools you can use to create Web pages; it's fine if they provide these tools as long as you can also create pages yourself. You must have control over the HTML in your pages.

✓ Use the company's traffic-analysis tool or, if you plan to use your own analysis tool, access the raw traffic logs. A log-analysis tool shows you how many people visit your site and how they get there. (These days many people use Google Analytics, Google's free stats program. As long as you can add a little piece of JavaScript to the bottom of every page, you can use Analytics; see www.google.com/analytics.)

You need to consider many issues when selecting a hosting company, most of which aren't directly related to the search engine issue. For my experience these two company has the best uptime hosting capacity,

1. Hostgator
2. Bluehost

## Domain

Search engines read uniform resource locators (URLs), looking for keywords in them. For instance, if you have a Web site with the domain name rodentracing.com and someone searches Google for rodent racing, Google sees rodent-racing as a match; because a dash appears between the two words, Google recognizes the words in the domain name. If, however, you run the words together (rodentracing).Google doesn't regard the individual words as individual words; it sees them as part of the same word.

That's not to say that Google can't find text within words — it can, and you sometimes see words on the search results pages partially bolded when Google does just that — but when ranking the page, Google doesn't regard the word it found inside another word as the same as finding the word itself.

To see this concept in action, use the allinurl: search syntax at Google. Type allinurl:rodent, for example, and Google finds URLs that contain the word rodent (including the directory names and filenames). So, putting keywords into the domain name and separating keywords with dashes provides a small benefit. Another advantage to adding dashes between words is that you can relatively easily come up with a domain name that's not already taken.

Although it may seem as though most of the good names were taken long ago, you can often come up with some kind of keyword phrase, separated with dashes, that's still available. Furthermore, search engines don't care which first-level domain you use; you can use .com, .net, .biz, .tv, or whatever; it doesn't matter. Now, having said all that, let me tell you my philosophy regarding domain names. In the search engine optimization field, it has become popular to use dashes and keywords in domain names, but in most cases, the lift provided by keywords in domain names is relatively small, and you should consider other, more important factors when choosing a domain name:

- ✓ A domain name should be short, easy to spell, and easy to remember.

It should also pass the radio test. Imagine that you're being interviewed on

the radio and want to tell listeners your URL. You want something that's instantly understandable without having to be spelled. You don't want to have to say "rodent dash racing dash events dot com"; it's better to say

"rodent racing events dot com."

- ✓ In almost all cases, you should get the .com version of a domain name. If the .com version is taken, do not try to use the .net or .org version for branding purposes! People remember .com, even if you say .org or .net or whatever. So, if you're planning to promote your Web site in print, on the radio, on TV, on billboards, and so on, you need the .com version.

A classic example is a situation involving Rent.com and Rent.net. These two different Web sites were owned by two different companies. Rent.net spent millions of dollars on advertising; every time I saw a Rent.net ad on a bus, I had to wonder how much of the traffic generated by these ads actually went to Rent.com! (Rent.net is now out of business — the domain name now points to Move.com — and Rent.com isn't.

 I don't know whether that's a coincidence!) Are keyworded domain names worth the trouble? Because the lift provided by keywords in the domain name may be rather small — and, in fact, putting too many keywords into a name can hurt your placement — you should probably focus on a single, brandable domain name (a .com version).

 On the other hand, you might register both versions. For instance, register both

Rodent-Racing-Events.com and RodentRacingEvents.com. Use RodentRacing-Events.com as the primary domain name, the one you want the search engines to see. Then do a 301 Redirect to point

RodentRacingEvents.com to Rodent-Racing-Events.com. (See Chapter 24 for information on the 301 Redirect.) That way, you can tell people to go to "rodent racing events dot com" without having to mention the dashes, yet the search engine will regard all links to either domain as pointing to the same site and will see the keywords rodent and racing in the domain name.

Don't use a domain-forwarding service for Web sites that you want to turn up in search engines. Many registrars now allow you to simply forward browsers to a particular site: A user types www.domain1.com, and the registrar forwards the browser to www.domain2.com, for instance. Such forwarding systems often use frames), which means that search engines don't index the site properly. Your site should be properly configured by using the name server settings, not a simple forward.

# Chapter 9 – Design Your Website

## Understanding the Very Basic Things

Just having a topic isn't enough — you need a purpose, too. The topic is merely what the site is about; the purpose is what the site does. Say, for example, that you want to create a site about penguins. Okay, that's a nice starting point. You like penguins — they're cute, unusual, and pretty interesting; many people share your interest in them. But why do you want to create a Web site about them? Do you have something to say? Do you have information to give, an opinion to share, or a particular point of view that you want to put across?

You don't need to have a PhD in aquatic ornithology to create such a site. Maybe you just like funny-looking birds that swim. But you still need a purpose, or the site just won't work out in the long run. Perhaps you spent ages plowing through the search engines, and you've gathered together the world's greatest collection of penguin links. But why did you go to all that trouble? What's your purpose?

If the purpose for creating a penguin site is for your own personal enjoyment, you really don't need to do much with the site. In fact, you can just create a Web page on your own hard drive or even settle for leaving the links in your Web browser's bookmarks. If you do want your page on the World Wide Web, however, you need to take into account the needs of your potential visitors, as well as your own needs for creating such a site.

Suppose you're putting your penguin page on the Web for the purpose of sharing everything you know about these birds with the world. How does that purpose change your approach to site design? You need to include more on the Web site than a bare list of links, for one thing. Everything you do with the site must help people understand its purpose. If you're setting up your own domain name, for example, you want to pick one that clearly describes your site's content — such as www.penguinfacts.com. (Grab it quick — it still wasn't taken at press time.)

The purpose of your site trickles down through each step you take in creating it. You want the title of each page in the site to specify how it supports the site's purpose. The textual content of each page needs to lead naturally into some specific aspect of the topic that furthers your goal. Each graphical image must be just the right one to drive home or emphasize a critical point.

Who are the people you expect to visit your site? What geographical or cultural groups do you want the site to appeal to? Without at least a general idea of your potential audience, you can't have much of an idea about what type of site to create.

If data is available about the audience for similar sites, you want to track it down. But where do you find it? Surprisingly, most of it's available from the people you're competing with. (Even if you're not running a commercial site, similar sites are your competitors.) Anyone who's been involved in any type of corporate intelligence work would be shocked at the way people on the World Wide Web casually throw around valuable information, instead of keeping it under lock and key.

Many sites offer links to their visitor data. Even a quick perusal of the server logs (which automatically record information about visitors) can provide you

with priceless insights into the sort of people who visit sites similar to the one you're creating. If the sites you want information on don't list links to their

log data, send an e-mail message to the Webmaster asking how to access it. Most Webmasters aren't the slightest bit security-conscious about their customer data, and you may be surprised at how many of them are more than willing to spill the beans about their visitors.

## Build & Keep Your Site Fresh

If your material never changes, the odds are pretty good that most people won't come back to it very often, if ever. Unless your sole topic is a rocksolid reference subject, you can't get away with anything less than constant updating. Sure, the Oxford English Dictionary can come out with a new edition only every few generations. (The first edition came out in 1928 and the second one in 1989, with only two supplements in between.) But such cases are very rare. Even if you deal with a modern high-tech equivalent, such as a site on the Java programming language or the current HTML standard, you need to stay on your toes.

If your core material is something that doesn't change often, you need to add some peripheral material that you can replace more frequently. Consider adding a Tip of the Day, fresh links, a Did You Know? column, or something along those lines so you can avoid offering only stale content to your return visitors.

How often you need to update your site depends partially on your topic and partially on your site policy. With sites that deal with volatile topics such as breaking international news, you need to update on an hourly basis at a minimum. On the other hand, sites that analyze the news can stand a more leisurely pace — daily, weekly, or even monthly — because their scope is considerably wider.

Even if your topic doesn't absolutely demand a certain update schedule, you should still establish a regular policy for how often you add fresh material to your site. Whatever schedule you establish, make sure you stick with it.

Remember the comfort factor and bear in mind that your site's visitors will be less comfortable if they don't know what to expect from you. Consistency on your side helps build trust on theirs.

A Web site must change at least once a month to keep visitors interested in coming back to it.

## Consistently Generated Content

When the World Wide Web first got started, it was pretty much a one-way street — Webmasters like you always made the decisions about what would appear and how it could be used. As the Web has evolved, however, it has taken on some important new characteristics.

Today, some of the Web's most popular sites aren't so much controlled by their Webmasters as they are by their users. Places like YouTube and MySpace are hotbeds for the users' self-expression — and, indeed, that is their reason for existence. The new trend that has led to the phrase "Web 2.0" is usergenerated content, supplemented by social networking.

Of course, the majority of Web sites are still generated almost totally by either individuals or small teams working together, but the public's hunger for its own chance to shine is seemingly insatiable — and it's something you might want to keep in mind as you design your own Web site. Wikipedia and the other wikis are collaborative efforts, and the old personal home page has largely given way to blogs — Web logs, or personalized diaries that can be syndicated and sent to others automatically.

## Make a Website Audience Will Love

The audience — which is made up of the visitors you hope to attract to your site

— determines the content. To set some basic limits, think of these visitors as being at a beginning, an intermediate, or an advanced level, and gauge your content accordingly. If you're aiming advanced content at a beginning audience or vice versa, you're looking at failure from the word go.

Not only does your audience determine your content, but its preferences influence your visual-design requirements as well. If your audience consists of high-school students whose interests revolve mainly around the latest musical sensations, you need a far different look from what you'd shoot for if it consists of retired naval officers who want to know about international events.

For the young music lovers, for example, you need to strike a tone that's lighthearted and exciting, both in your words and graphics. Brighter colors and a more relaxed and informal tone for the text are the call here. For the old salts, though, you need to take a heavier approach, with darker, duller colors and a middling-formal approach to language.

Whatever the group you're aiming for, ask yourself the following questions:

✓ How do they communicate with one another? Roller-hockey players don't communicate quite the same way as cartographers do. What are the level and style of language usage in the group? Do its members have a particular jargon, slang, or regional dialect? If so, can you use it comfortably and correctly?

✓ What kind and color of clothes do they wear? This kind of information tells you volumes about their preferences.

People who are willing to wear suits and ties in midsummer don't think the same way as those who prefer casual clothing. The colors they wear also indicate the color ranges they're likely to feel comfortable with on your site.

✓ What's their worldview? For many people, the world consists of their apartment or house; the road between it and their workplace; their cubicle, office, or factory floor; and a couple of restaurants somewhere along that pathway. For others, the world consists only of Wall Street and the Asian financial markets. For some, the world is a series of airports, cell phones, and e-mail messages. Anything that exists outside your audience's worldview is invisible to them and probably doesn't belong on your Web site.

Find out all that you can — from what kind of cars your visitors drive to the hours they wake and sleep. Any kind of information you can nail down about your visitors and their lives helps you to understand them — and that understanding can't help but improve your site's appeal.

# Chapter 10 – Turn Your Website Into Money Making matchine

If you're tired of slow search response times, try AlltheWeb. It gives you answers so fast that your head spins.

To make sure that people know your Web site exists, you should have it listed in lots of search engines. How many you should list it in is a matter of opinion. There's certainly no harm in going for broke and listing your site with every search engine, but about a zillion of them are out there — and most of them aren't nearly as well known as Yahoo! or Google. In my opinion, after you're listed with all the ones in Table 13-1, any more effort runs into the law of diminishing returns. Yes, you will generate more visits by listing your site at even more search sites, but you don't get anywhere near as many visits from obscure search sites as you do from the more popular ones.

Speaking of popularity, the number one search engine is the oddly named but fantastically functional Google (www.google.com). Not that it needs the push, but I highly recommend it. If your site isn't listed on Google, you'll miss out on a lot of potential visitors.

There are many reasons for Google's success, but the main one is simply that it gives better results than many of its competitors. This is in large part due to its sophisticated page-analysis software, and you would do well to keep in mind what it looks for when you design your site's pages. Here are some tips on how to do that:

✓   Make sure that the important terms describing your site (the ones you think people will use as search terms when they're hunting for information on Google) appear in both your page title and in the first paragraph of your Web page.

✓   Use the same words at least a few times elsewhere on the page, but don't go hog wild — if you overdo it, you'll lower your ranking.

✓   Break up your page's text by using heading elements (H1, H2, and so on) that contain key phrases. Google pays more attention to these than to normal text.

✓ If, for some reason, your page design can't utilize heading elements, use the B (bold text) element to emphasize your keywords. (The STRONG element does the same thing.)

✓ Exchange links with other Webmasters, especially with those who already have a high Google ranking.

Using search sites isn't the only way of getting the word out. You can also work out reciprocal link arrangements with other Web sites, either on a personal level or through the agency of a banner-link exchange.

## Using Keyword into Pages

Search sites have different ways of gathering information on the content of Web sites:

✓ Some search sites are put together by human effort. People visit Web sites that have been submitted to the search site and then manually categorize those sites.

✓ Other search sites are fully automated. Programs called robots or spiders surf the Web, cataloging their findings and adding Web pages to the search site's database. Robots and spiders don't just note the URL of a page, though. They also index all the words on the page (except for words like a, an, the, for, and so on).

When someone runs a search, the search terms are compared with the indexed words. Links to whatever sites match the search terms are then shown to the person doing the searching.

In addition to the words in the text of your page (and sometimes in the alt text fields of images and other elements as well), search engines also index meta keywords.

The following sections give you the lowdown on incorporating keywords into your site.

## Adding Meta Data

META is one of the most versatile elements in HTML because it's one of the most poorly defined ones. Some would just say it doesn't have many limits. Its name and content attributes enable you to put many types of information into your HTML documents.

META always goes within the HEAD element, and it has no end tag. You can have all the META elements you want, but only two of its uses matter to a search engine: as a page description and as a list of keywords. Neither one is essential. In fact, despite the frenzy about META keywords, your page description and TITLE element are actually more useful for search engines.

(Google, the most successful search engine, doesn't even look at

META keywords.)

## Page description

When someone performs a search that returns a hit to your site, the response usually shows your page title and a blurb of text from the beginning of your page. This response underscores the importance of a good title. If the first sentence of your page doesn't describe all its contents, that may not be the best possible enticement for someone to visit it. If your page has a META description, however, the search engine will use that description to — you guessed it — describe your page.

Imagine that you have a page titled "The Love Letters of Grover Cleveland." Well, that title may not mean much to a lot of folks, and if the first sentence is something like a tame quotation from one of those letters, you're not doing too well. But a good description like this can fix that:

<META name="description" content="The secret life of the 24th President"> **List of keywords**

You add keywords in much the same way that you add a description:

<META name="keywords" content="Grover Cleveland, 24th President,

Buffalo, New York, Mugwumps">

Mugwumps? Trust me — it's a Grover Cleveland thing.

The META keywords aren't that important because the content of the page itself should already have the important terms in it. And some search engines don't even look at META keywords. Where keywords are useful is in a special situation that you can't easily accommodate in the visible page content without looking silly: You need to intentionally misspell words.

It's a fact: Lots of people have trouble spelling or typing or both. Therefore you should also add common spelling errors to your list of keywords. For example, if you list flying saucers and someone's looking for flying sossers, that person won't be able to find your site. (Well, okay, you may not want that person to find you, but I'm not going to get into that.) You should also cover yourself for any legitimate spelling variants. For example, if you sell tires and don't want to miss out on the British market, you should also list tyres among your keywords.

When it comes to choosing keywords, don't neglect synonyms. One person may look for car parts while another searches for automotive accessories

## Adjusting Keyword in the Content

The actual content of your Web pages is much more important than META keywords. In fact, it's critical — to both your search-engine ranking and visitor retention. When you write the copy for your pages, make sure that you throw in as many terms as possible that accurately describe your topic. As far as the search engines are concerned, the more often you can reasonably include relevant keywords, the better. After all, search engines rank your Web site by how well the contents of your pages match up with the search term that someone enters.

When it comes to the human visitors to your pages, as opposed to the robotic visitors, you need to write in a way that entertains your audience. As a professional writer, I always try to avoid using the same phrase too often. When I need to refer to the same thing or action over and over again, I strive to find new ways to say it. I practically live for synonyms and pronouns.

1. To start with, make up a list of terms that you think people might use if they search for your page.

2. Go ahead and write your content without paying any attention to your list.

3. After you've finished writing your page, look over the list and mark down how many times you've used each of the terms on the page.

4. Go over your page and see where you can work in the words that you didn't use. Then for words that you did use, look for places you might use them again without screwing up the flow of the writing.

After you've done these things, toss the list in the trash and reread your page. If it's still good, go with it. If it doesn't read well, you may have to sacrifice some of the terms to make the text more reader-friendly.

## Analyzing Competitor Keyword

Taking a look at what other people are doing with keywords can be instructive. You can find out just what people are searching for plenty of ways; if some of those terms fit in with what you're doing, you may want to work them in. Here are some ways to analyze keywords:

✓ Keyword Analysis Tool: One of the best sites you can visit is Keyword Analysis Tool, shown in Figure 13-1. It runs a check on sites you specify.

✓ Keyword Extractor: Check out Keyword Extractor, a useful freebie from AnalogX (see Figure 13-2). You can find it at http://www.analogx.com/contents/download/Network/keyex/Freeware.htm. Keyword Extractor lets you analyze Web pages just like search engines do. It indexes all the words on the page and assigns weights to them depending on their frequency of use and position on the page.

One of the best ways to use this program is to perform a search at one of the major search sites, follow the links to the top-ranked pages, and run Keyword Extractor on each of those pages. Study the results to see how those pages earned their ranks.

# Chapter 11 - Start Advertising More Products & Earn little more Money

Advertising on your blog has never been easier. Many different advertising systems offer bloggers a free way to place ads on their blogs, and businesses have picked up on the fact that blog advertising can really work. Putting an ad or two on your blog can help you easily earn a little money doing something you enjoy. Many bloggers turn a pretty penny, and some even earn a living, from advertising.

Ever since websites came into existence, you could find online advertisements. From the first web banners of the early Internet to today's contextual advertising systems, ads have run the gamut from wildly successful to a waste of precious bandwidth. In some cases, the effectiveness of ads has more to do with the readers than anything else.

On the blog for some topics, blog readers willingly look at ads and even click them, but audiences on other blogs just don't have the patience to wade through advertisements that clutter their reading pleasure. So, you need to know what your audience will tolerate before you make a big play with ads! Turning your blog into a retirement savings plan won't happen overnight, and don't take the addition of advertisements to the average blog lightly. It all requires planning, patience, and faith and trust in your readership. Depending on your audience, you might even need to request input from them about the advertisements that you choose to deploy on your blog.

## Let's See How Advertisement Works

Banner ads (rectangular ads usually placed along the top of a site) used to dominate ad slots on the web but have become less important because people often just tune them out. Then, pop-up, animated, and blinking advertisements generated a few clicks and ultimately managed to generate a massive

backlash. Many of these moving, beeping, and blinking ads just irritated users, instead of successfully advertising.

Today's contextual advertising tools are actually intelligent; ads are matched by subject to the words and phrases that you use on your blog. Generally, this approach gives you ads that better suit your readers' interests, making those readers more likely to click the ads. First, decide whether your blog is meant for an advertising campaign. Many blogs can benefit greatly from advertisements. However, you should think about a few things before diving in:

- ✓ Does your blog have a design that's ready for ads?

- ✓ Does your blog software support the advertising system you choose?

- ✓ Will advertising earn you any money?

- ✓ Will your audience put up with ads?

Answering these questions isn't easy; in fact, you might find it impossible unless you jump in. Try using some advertising and observe the results.

## Make an Organized Plan for Advertising

You can use several kinds of advertising methods to turn a blog into a place where you can make a tidy profit. The last few years have seen an explosion of companies that want a piece of the action in the blogosphere, and these companies have come up with creative ways to make ads easy to use, simple to implement, and appealing to your readers.

If you're a new blogger or just new to advertising programs, you can easily latch onto the first advertising system that you find and commit to using it. Although this system may serve your needs well, you might want to take a look at some of the different ad systems available and find out about how advertising tends to work in the blogosphere before you start using ads.

While you do your research, keep in mind that if you decide to make that leap into monetizing your blog, you should choose software that allows you to control your advertising so that it doesn't overwhelm the blog audience that you worked so hard to build.

A multitude of advertising companies offer bloggers simple solutions to monetize websites. Most of these programs work in similar ways but have unique delivery methods. Advertising programs range from text-only ads to flashy animations, and even full-page advertisements that really get your readers' attention! As a blogger, choosing an advertising program that works for your audience can make the difference between an increase in readers and turning off your existing traffic.

## Which Format You Use?

You can deliver ads to a blog audience in four different ways. Additional methods are available, but most don't work very well in a blog. The most popular advertisement formats for blogs are,

✓ Text-based ads: These ads are text-only and feature a link or links to the advertiser's website or service. Each ad is very plain, and most advertising systems limit your ability to customize their look and feel. ✓ Graphical banner and button ads: Banner and button ads can be static or animated images. These ads usually have preset sizes, but you can customize them to fit your blog design.

✓ RSS ads: Ads are a new addition to RSS feeds; while the format has taken off with the public, advertisers have jumped on the bandwagon. Such ads can include text or images, and they're linked to the advertiser's website straight from your RSS feed. See how this kind of advertising looks when someone views the RSS feed in a newsreader, shown in Figure 18-1.

✓ Pop-up ads: Pop-ups tend to be everyone's least favorite type of ad, but oddly enough, pop-up ads that open in a new window are still quite successful at getting people to click an advertiser's website. The readers might be fairly irritated by the time they get to the site, but they do click.

The Interactive Advertising Bureau makes recommendations each year about ad sizes and standards. You might find the recommendations useful in planning for ads. Visit www.iab.net/standards/adunits.asp to see the options. Most ad programs today — with the exception of sponsorships — use contextual advertising, which coordinates ad display with related editorial content.

So, a blog post about skiing might include ads for ski shops and resorts. A blogger who posts about blogging, for example, ends up with ads for blog software and tools. (I speak from experience here.) Contextual ad systems search your blog for keywords that match products the advertisers have in their inventory. These ads then appear beside the topic keywords and, in theory, apply in the context of the web page on which they appear.

## Let's See Some of the Business Model

Money can flow from the advertiser to the blogger in different ways. Always read the terms of service for an ad program because each advertising company has a different idea about how to compensate bloggers. The usual business models for online ads are,

✓ Cost per impression: In this model, advertisers pay for the number of times a computer loads a page that displays the ad. The advertiser might prefer that a reader click its ad, but it recognizes that simply appearing on a blog that users access also has value.

✓ Cost per click or pay per click: The blogger makes money only when a reader clicks an ad and goes to the advertiser's website. This type of ad is very common in contextual ad programs, as well as on search engines in the sponsored results section.

- ✓ Cost per action: The advertiser pays only when the reader actually takes action after he or she views and clicks the ad on the blog. This required action can include anything from signing up to receive more information to actually purchasing a product.

- ✓ Sponsorships: When an advertiser wants to be actively associated with the content of your blog, it might offer to sponsor the blog or some part of the blog. A sponsorship usually includes premium advertisements and exclusive ad placement, and the blogger sometimes even thanks the sponsor in the editorial content of the site.

A lot of bloggers have had the same great idea about the ads on their blogs:

"I'll just click these myself and send my cost-per-click rates through the roof! I'll make millions!" Unfortunately, the advertising companies have figured out this little scheme, and they refer to it as click fraud.

Advertisers spend good money to have their ads displayed, and companies that run advertisement programs go out of their way to make sure that clicks on those ads are legitimate clicks. Make sure that you understand what happens if you click ads on your own blog before you do it: Some programs penalize or even ban bloggers who engage in click fraud.

## Keep Going

Most bloggers choose to incorporate advertising programs by signing up with a company that serves as a middleman between the blogger and the advertiser. This company typically negotiates rates with the advertiser, tracks ad performance, and pays the blogger for advertising placement. Although you can cut out the middleman and sell your own ad space, many bloggers find that they don't really want to spend their time dealing with the negotiation, tracking, and technical overhead.

But even the most time-pressed blogger can likely find the strength to listen when an advertiser contacts that blogger directly and offers to sponsor the blog. These arrangements are typically more lucrative for the blogger (and the advertiser, presumably), and the two parties negotiate this relationship on a case-by-case basis, depending on the audience, product, blog traffic, and other factors. After you decide on formats, placement, and business models, it's time to put ads on your blog. The good — and bad — news is that you have dozens of options to choose from. In the following sections, I show you a few well regarded advertising programs to consider.

## Introducing Google Adsense

AdSense is Google's contextual advertising program, and it's really the biggest player in the contextual advertising arena. When you sign up for Google AdSense, you choose what kinds of ads you want on your blog, from text to images to videos. You can see examples of the Google AdSense formats in Figure 18-3. Advertisers pay Google money when your blog visitors click the advertisements displayed beside your content, and you receive a portion of those payments. Successful bloggers who have a lot of traffic can earn a living from Google AdSense, but income varies greatly, depending on the size of your audience and how well your blog topics match the advertisers who contract with Google.

## Text Link Ads

Based in New York, Text Link Ads is one of the most popular and recognizable advertising systems used by bloggers. Designed with blogs in mind, these ads are a slightly different option than contextual advertising programs that try to relate ads specifically to your content. Instead, you get only simple links that you preapprove, which are related but much lower-key in look and feel than contextual ads. You can display Text Link Ads on the same page with Google AdSense, Yahoo! Publisher Network, and other contextually served ads.

## Ad-Brite Another Ad Network Like Google

AdBrite is an advertising marketplace similar to the others mentioned in the preceding sections. Bloggers can choose between text, banner ads, full page interstitials (splash pages containing a full-page advertisement), inline ads, and image ads. Interstitials are high-paying ads that take over the entire browser window when a user clicks to move from one page of your website to another; they usually feature a Skip This Ad link or button.

## How You Can Put Ad on Your Website/Blog

To get these ads onto your website, most often, the programs you sign up for provide you with a bit of code that you insert into your website templates. Some programs have step-by-step instructions for popular blog software packages, but be aware that you might also need to consult your blog software documentation for help with putting your ads where you want them. First, decide just where you want the ads on your page. The best thing to do when you're thinking about introducing ads into your blog design is to make sure the ads aren't overpowering. Don't damage your reputation or credibility by overloading the site with ads or by associating ads too closely with your blog posts and content.

Aside from pop-up ads, nothing is more annoying than having a blog design that's created around ads rather than a blog that's designed to include ads. At the same time, you need to place ads in spots where readers can see them. Bloggers have discovered a few truths about ads, although your results might differ:

✓ Ads at the top and bottom of each page do poorly. Readers often ignore and rarely view advertisements along the top or the bottom of a blog because the site content usually appears in the middle of the screen. While users scroll their windows to view site content, they may never see these top and bottom advertisements at all.

✓ Ads in the sidebars perform well but might interfere with navigation. The left side of the website is a traditional place for ads. However, it's also a prime place for navigation tools, and your website design might require that you locate such tools higher than the ads you want people to view. As for the right side, not only are navigation tools sometimes placed here, but the bulk of blog content tends be aligned to the left side of the screen. Some users might cover the right side with other windows and therefore miss these rightside advertisements entirely.

✓ Ads within the content itself get clicked. Some blogs have their ads placed within their content, and therefore visitors don't miss the ads. But you need to be careful when you use advertising within your content. Remember that you want to make the content king, not the ad.

Try out ads in different places on your blog and see how your audience reacts, as well as how your earnings do. You might need to try several different locations before you find one that balances your readers' needs with your advertisers'.

## Want to Try another Affiliate Site from ClickBank

If you ever blogged about a product that you really like and just knew that you were helping the company that makes the product make a sale, you can now make some money from that sale with affiliate marketing. Popular retailers have set up affiliate marketing programs, most notably Amazon.com. You sign up with an affiliate program, and when you blog about one of its products, you include a piece of identifying information that the company gives you. You earn cash when readers of your blog click the product and buy it. If you find yourself blogging about items that others might buy as a result of your recommendation, check to see whether the company that makes the product

has an affiliate program and sign yourself up. In short order, your blog can contain links to books, DVDs, or other products that provide you with a commission on each product bought through a link from your website.

## Amazon Associates

Amazon is the most recognized affiliate program available, and it's arguably one that you likely benefit from using because many bloggers mention books and DVDs that they've enjoyed. Amazon Associates works by letting you create specially formatted links that you can use on your blog to drive traffic to the Amazon website. Anything that a visitor who clicks your link purchases earns you a percentage of the sale as a referral fee just like Clickbank product we choose earlier in the book.

## LinkShare

LinkShare is another affiliate program that calls itself a pay-per-action marketing network. You can place both text and graphical ads on your blog and make money from any sales that come from readers' purchases.

## Google Affiliate Network

If you regularly blog about consumer products, the Google Affiliate Network can help you turn those blog posts into money. Sign up to review the advertisers participating in the network, and learn how to track conversions of your recommendations into purchases. Many well-known brands participate in the Google Affiliate Network, from Target to Verizon.

# Chapter 12 - How to Drive Easy & Quality Traffic in Your Website

You set up a website. Design it wonderfully and have a product for promoting. Now you have to drive traffic into your blog/website. Traffic is the most important part when we are talking about affiliate marketing and wanted to earn some real cash from the foundation we are creating in previous 8 chapters.

So why traffic so important? Just think, you set up a website and also create tons of related content according to your site. But if you don't have traffic then how can you sell the affiliate products or service you are advertising in your site.

The good thing if you follow the each and every step we discuss in the previous sections. Then I can guarantee you that traffic will be coming into your website. But there is some requirements, you have to write 15-20 relevant, high quality, unique content. Your content has to be more than 500 words and you have to maintain the keyword strategy I taught you.

There were more than 100 ways you can drive traffic into your website, but we will only focus in these technique which one is much easier when you are just starting SEO or affiliate marketing.

## Article Marketing

When you are using article marketing, you can promote your website in many different ways. Not only does the article marketing have the ability to attract readers who can be directed to your site due to the links that are provided in the article, but it also has the ability to build up your status in the search engines due to link backs and SEO content. Article marketing is the best way to use SEO for your website.

There are many article hubs where you can post articles for free online. They are easy to use as you can submit your articles to them and have them go live. Most of them have certain restrictions regarding article length that you will have to comply with when you are submitting articles. They will allow you to post a link to the website at the end of the article. In some cases, you can put a hyperlink right into an article, although most article hubs will discourage any hyper linking. For the most part, the links are found at the end of the articles in a reference box.

The articles must be search engine optimized so that they can be found on the search engines. The articles should contain about 2-3 percent of keyword density and also a link to the website that is placed at the end.

Some rules to follow when you are using article marketing in your SEO project are as follows:

- Make the articles short but not too short - 400 words is best for the attention span of those online;
- Use no more than 4 percent density when it comes to keywords;
- Use the keywords in the title of the article and the first sentence;
- Use the reference box to put the link in for the article;
- Make sure that you have no broken links in your reference box;
- Do not overuse the keywords as this will get the article rejected;   Come up

with two or three keywords to use in an article;
- Use a site that will spread the articles all over the internet.

One site that you may want to try for article marketing is [www.ezinearticles.com](www.ezinearticles.com). This site allows you to post up to 10 free articles with links back to your site. You must follow the terms of the site in order to get your articles posted.

Like most article hubs that will eventually distribute the articles all over the internet,

Ezine will want to make sure that you are writing an informative, well written article. The article should not contain any typos or spelling errors. You should check your grammar when you are writing your article to make sure that what you have written is grammatically correct. You do not have to shoot for Hemingway style writing when you are trying to have an article published online, but you should shoot for reasonable quality.

   Do not overstuff keywords as this will get your article kicked back. Use the keywords as directed and not more than 4 times for a 400 word article. Take a look at other repetitive words that you may be using in your articles and keep those to a minimum as well, even if they are not related to your original choice in keywords. You may, for example, be selling wedding shower bridal favors but will find that using "wedding showers" more than four times will get your article bounced back for excessive keyword usage.

Take the time to fix any articles that do not meet the requirements. Most article hubs will help you out by telling you what is wrong with your articles. You can learn how to create articles that will help out your website when using article marketing in this way.

Your articles that you use must be original. You cannot steal the articles from someone else, change a few words and put your name on them. Article hubs run the articles through a check system to see if they appear anywhere else online. If they do, then they will bounce it back to you and the article will be rejected. Make sure that all of the articles that you use for article marketing are original.

Articles should be informative and not promotional at all. While some article hubs like Ezine allow for reviews of products, product reviews have to be non-partial and not read like a promotional piece. Your articles should all be information pieces that are designed to inform the public of a product or service without seeming to advertise anything.

Going back to the idea of a site for high heeled shoes, articles would be written for such a site as to discuss the positive aspects of wearing high heeled shoes, without any negative references. Some good ideas for article marketing for such a site would be the following titles of articles:

- Why Your Legs Look Better Wearing High Heeled Shoes  High Heeled Shoes - What Are The Trends For Today?
- How To Buy High Heeled Shoes Online

Each of these articles would be information pieces that would discuss the benefits of wearing high heeled shoes and buying them online without seeming to be overtly promotional. Remember that you want to keep your articles from any negative aspects about your product, but also not make it appear as if you are merely trying to advertise the product. Think of "how" and "why" when you are considering titles for your articles.

Remember that they should be informative articles that will help the public learn something that is relevant to your product.

All of the articles should be relevant to your product in a positive way and should give the public information that they will want to know. You can submit your articles yourself to free article hubs, or you can use an article submission service that can promote your articles for you.

There are two main reasons why people use article marketing online. They are:

- The SEO used in the articles can attract a potential customer who will click on the link;
- They establish links to your site and raise your status in the search engine results pages.

Of these two reasons, the latter is why most people choose to use article marketing online. While it is possible that someone would see your article and then click on the link to purchase the product that you are promoting, the main reason you should look to article marketing is to promote link building to your site.

There are many article hubs online that will offer you a chance to put your article online for free. You can find a list of free article marketing sites by going online and doing a search for them through Google. You can also use a site like [www.articlemarketer.com](www.articlemarketer.com) to distribute articles online in this way. You pay a fee for article marketer, but you do not have to manually submit the articles as this site will do it all for you.

Article marketing is one of the best ways to get your product and service well known. Whether you are selling a product, service or even an idea, you can benefit by marketing it online in this manner. You do need to make sure that all of your articles are search engine optimized for your website. Once you start marketing articles online in this manner, you will see how easy it is to write and promote yourself online.

If you do not know how to write articles or do not want to take the time to do so, you can promote yourself by hiring a copywriter to write your articles

and distribute them online for you. Many of those who want to market their sites will pay a copywriter to write the articles for them. Some copywriters will also distribute the articles for you at a slight additional charge.

## Using SEO In Press Releases

Press releases are yet another way that you can use SEO for your website. Like everything else that you write and distribute online, the press releases should be search engine optimized with keywords. You will want to follow some of the same rules when it comes to keywords and density as you did for the articles marketing with some differences.

Just as there are free article hubs to distribute articles for online, there are also free sites that will allow you to distribute press releases. A press release is a promotional writing about your company that comes off like a news article. You should have something new or exciting that you are announcing in your press release that makes it "news" worthy.

Using the shoes example again, one of the titles for a good press release would be "Fall Ushers In New Styles In High Heeled Shoes." As is the case with other products that you write for online venues, you want to use the keywords that you have chosen in the title of the press release.

Your press release should be timely and current. It can relate to a special sale that you are having or new arrivals that are not even really "new." You can use your imagination to make just about anything on your site seem to be new and exciting.

You have to follow the submission rules for press releases just as you would for article marketing. Press releases have to have the city and state where you are writing from as well as the name of your company. Unlike articles where you put a live link into a resource box, you can provide the link at the end of the press release along with other information, such as an 800 number if you have one.

There are not as many free press release sites where you can post your press releases as there are article marketing sites, but there are many free sites to use. You can do a Google search to find a press release site or free sites where you can distribute your free press releases. You can distribute the same press release to more than one site.

You should make your press release sound like a news article, complete with quotes in the article that will make it sound more authentic. The press release should be written in the third person but quote the owner of the company or some other executive in first person. If you do not want to use your name in the press release, you can use a false name. You want to be consistent when you are writing your press releases and using names.

While you can punch up a promotional angle when you are writing a press release, you still want to keep the piece informative. You should use the same SEO rules when you are distributing a press release as you would when you are distributing a news article. Make sure that you do not go overboard with the keywords.

Again, the purpose of using the free press release distribution using SEO is to distribute more links online. The more links that you distribute, the more your site will rise in ranking in the search engine results pages. As you want to continue to make your site rise high in the search engines, you will want to take advantage of all of the opportunities there are online to raise your rankings. Press releases should be used just as article marketing should be used for SEO content.

You also have the chance of someone seeing your press release online and then contacting your company about the offer. If you have a limited time offer for your product, you should note this in the press release. Unlike articles, press releases are dated. They can be a free way to promote a special sale that you have coming up or to hail in a new product or service.

## Using SEO+Video Ads

One way that you can get promotion for your website is to use SEO for video ads. Video ads are hotter than ever and will come up higher in the search engine results pages than text. For this reason, many people are posting video ads on free sites such as [www.youtube.com](www.youtube.com) so that they can get some exposure for their website.

Like everything else that you do when you are promoting your site using SEO, you have to make sure that video ads are search engine optimized. There are tags that are available to name video ads. You need to make use of these tags so that you can add keywords and have the video come up in the search engines.

You should not underestimate the importance of using video in your ads. Video is displayed more predominantly on the search engine results pages and is a very important aspect of website marketing. You can easily draw up your own video ad using a camcorder and upload it online. Many of those who have video ads online use only sound with a video design for their ad. This still gives the video preference in the search engines.

Using a video script, you can create a video ad that is accompanied by music and graphic designs. You can then tag it with a keyword that is related to your site as well as put the name of your website on the site where you distribute the video. This gives you SEO exposure on the video sites as

well. There are several sites where you can upload video ads including YouTube. Take a look online and search out the sites where you can upload free video and then use it to promote your website.

If you are looking for a way to get your website out to the masses using SEO strategies, take a look at what video can do for you. Because computer technology has come such a long way in recent years, it is now easier than ever to promote yourself using video ads.

Always remember to use keywords accordingly when you are using video promotions.

## Blogging with SEO Marketing

One of the easiest ways that you can promote your website for free with SEO content and links is to use blogging. Most websites today have blogs that are connected to them. These blogs are the easiest way to update the site so that it stays current in the search engines.

The search engines are not only looking for keyword rich content when they send out their search engine bots for search engine ranking, but also constant content. The content on your website should not get stale. This can end up costing you ranking in the search engines and also end up costing you sales.

If you have a website that has been carefully constructed (again, we will use the example of the shoes website) and want to make sure that it is updated without having to re-do the website all of the time, the best way to do so is to use a blog.

You can go to a site called [www.wordpress.com](www.wordpress.com) to get started in your own blog. The blogs created by this site can be used to connect to your own website.

Once you have created a blog, you can then use SEO rich content to put in the blog on a daily basis. Blogs are different than articles in writing style, formality and information.

Blogs can be written in the first person style. Many blogs are written as narrative prose rather than informative third person writing. You can alternate between styles if you so choose to get the information into your blogs.

By changing your blog on a daily basis, you can keep your website up to date. This will continue to keep it ranking high in the search engine rankings. You will also be adding links that will boost it in the search engines as well.

Blog writing is very simple and can be accomplished in a few short lines. You do not have to use very long blogs to get your point across. All of your blogs, however, should be relevant to your website.

When you use some blog software, you can add links into your blogs. These links can be added using HTML or in some cases, just using the tools on the toolbar. If you have your blog attached to your website, you can then just add to the blog all of the time. You can display more than one blog on your website.

The more links that you continue to distribute throughout the internet, the higher your site will rank in the search engines. You will want to make sure that you use the links in all of your blogs for your website. This will give you more links that will ultimately lead back to your site and raise search engine rankings.

Another site that you may want to consider when you are looking for informal SEO for your website is Squidoo. This is found at [www.squidoo.com](www.squidoo.com) and allows you to post photos, information about your website and links right onto the site. You can make this into your daily blog by using an RSS feed that you incorporate into the site to keep it updated.

It is very important that you continue to keep your website updated when you are using SEO and marketing concepts to try to make sure that your site does not get lost amid the many in the search engines. Blogs are an informal and fun way that you can keep your website updated and ranking high in the search engines.

## Exchange Links

This is a sure and proven method. Rarely would you see a site where there is no link to another site. Many webmasters are willing to exchange links with one another so that they could produce more public awareness about their sites. You'll soon see and feel the sudden upsurge of the traffic coming in to your site from other sites.

A major prerequisite in exchanging links with other sites is having the same niche or content as the other site. They should share a common subject so that there is continuity in the providing of service and information to what interests your target traffic.

Exchanging links also boosts your chances of getting a high ranking in Search Engine results. It is common knowledge that Search Engines ranks high sites that have inbound and outbound theme-related links. With a good ranking position in the Search Engines, you will generate more traffic in your website without the high costs.

## Traffic Exchange

This is like exchanging links but on a different higher level. This may cost a bit more than exchanging or trading links but could be made cheaper because you get to earn credits. You can use those credits when viewing others traffic, while you earn credits when someone views yours.

Traffic exchange services are the viewing of another's site or page. This is done vice versa where a site can use your sites contents and so can you to his or her site. You both benefit from each other's efforts to generate traffic. The other sites visitors can go to your pages and know more about your site as well as theirs. Once again the public awareness of your sites existence is boosted.

## Write and Submit Articles

There are many E-zines and online encyclopedias in the Internet which provides free space for articles to be submitted. If you want to save costs, you can do the articles yourself. There are many freelance writers who are willing to write for you for a small fee, but to save money, it is wise to do those articles yourself.

Write articles that are themed along with the niche of your site. Write something that you have expertise on so that when they read it, they can feel your knowledge about the subject and will be eager to go to your site. Write articles that produce tips and guidelines to the subject or niche your site has. Include a resource box at the end of your article that can link them to your site.

Write a little about yourself and your site. If you provide a light, information-laden and interesting article, they will go to your site for more. If you want to leverage on article submission, you can try paid services like http://www.articlemarketer.com/.

## Google Adwords to Drive Laser Targeted Traffic

This is a reason why E-commerce site laser target certain groups of people and drive them to their site to showcase their sites and products. Precision marketing is essential so that you could count on all the traffic on your site as potential customers.

It's a common business notion that if you want to make money, you have to spend money. One good way of spending money for business gain is through advertising. Advertising brings in the people because through advertising, they know that there is such a company or product in existence. With the right type of advertising, you can see the spurt of traffic growth to your site. With a high volume of traffic, even if only a small portion or percentage turns out to be buying customers it is still a good average of profit generating income.

Right now, there is no other advertising scheme that would be worth every cent than using Google's Adwords (http://www.adwords.com/). The surge in popularity of Google's Adwords is very evident as you can see so many sites sporting this ad scheme.

In using Google's Adwords, you pay a certain fee depending on the number of keywords your ad is keyword sensitive to. Each time a person does a search in Google, the keyword or keywords use generate ads in the side of Google which are generated by the keywords they have assigned for their ads.

This method laser targets the traffic a site wants for their site. This also ensures that you are readily visible in the first page of a search result. Paying Google for this ad scheme ensures that your target group of people sees your ads. You drive your laser targeted traffic to your site which provides for their needs and wants. You can also be sure that you can meet their demands and needs.

Aside from Google, you can also be featured in their other search networks, these includes sites like, AskJeeves, AOL Search and Netscape. These sites also show Adwords ads that react to searches done by visitors.

There are also content networks, non-Search Engine sites that feature Google Adwords, which will also carry your ads. But this is subjected to the niche the site features. Your chosen keywords will determine which content network shall feature your ad. The frequency of your ad shall also be determined by your allowed budget.

To get a good number or estimate of the traffic to buying customer ratio it is good to laser target your traffic. Knowing that your traffic are all potential customers and are interested in your products and company provides you with a more accurate statistics. This will show you how effective your utilizing of Google Adwords is.

Drive laser targeted traffic to your site by using keywords or keyword phrases for your Goggle Adwords that pertains to your company and to your products. There are many online Internet tools that can help you in choosing keywords and keyword phrases that are currently in demand that could help drive laser targeted traffic to your site.

With your Google Adwords ad, you are ensured that every click to your ad is a potential customer that is precisely looking pr interested in what you have to offer. Make sure that your Google Adwords ad has the right keywords so that you can drive you're laser targeted traffic to your site.

Using Google Adwords to help boost the drive to increase laser targeted traffic will prove to be very beneficial as many other companies can attest to. The benefits are high with the cost relatively justifiable.

## Using A SEO Company

Many businesses and others who are seeking a way of getting the message of their website out there to the public are using companies that specialize in SEO marketing in order to get the job done.

SEO companies specialize in internet marketing and will do the following in order to get a website optimized for the internet:

- Research keywords;
- Restructure the existing text (if any) on the website so it is SEO;
- Create pictures, video and tags;
- Create a blog and keep it updated using SEO content; Use article marketing;
- Create press releases using SEO marketing.

The SEO company will work with the website to make sure that they are helping them gain in the search engine results pages. Most companies will be able to tell a business where they are currently ranking in the search engine results pages of the main search engines.

Once the company tells the business where they rank, they will then give them an estimate, based upon experience, as to how far they can help the company rise within the search engine results page rankings.

The rise in the search engine rankings begins right away and can start as soon as the company starts to promote the website. In most cases, there will be an immediate improvement when it comes to ranking as the SEO company pays attention to the vital keywords that are needed to boost the website in page rankings.

It will take many months, however, before link building and SEO can work together to bring the website to the forefront of the search engine results pages.

Businesses that are seeking an SEO company to boost them in the search engines should be sure that the company can provide them with what type of results they can expect and where.

Be sure that you deal with a company that has experience in the SEO world and will not be using any black hat tricks to boost up the rankings. These tactics, such as using link farms and link spamming, can end up getting your site banned from the search engines. Deal with companies that use natural building tactics and white hat SEO to boost up your rankings in the search engines.

Another factor to look at when you are seeking out a company that can help you with

SEO is where they promise to boost your rankings. Some companies will purchase small search engines that no one uses in order to promise clients top spots in search engine results pages. You need to have a top spot in the main search engines that others are using, namely Google, Yahoo and MSN.

The decision on whether or not you decide to use an SEO company depends upon how much time you have to invest in helping your business gain in the search engines. If you can commit to writing articles, blogs and press releases on a regular basis and monitoring the search engine results, you can perform your own SEO. You just need to follow the examples in this book in order to do so.

However, if you find that you are not prepared to put that much time into an SEO marketing project, you may find that you are better off to hire an SEO company that will be able to give you the service that you need.

A good SEO company has experience in all aspects of internet marketing and is prepared to work with your site to boost it up. While you may start to see positive results right away when it comes to the efforts on behalf of the marketing company, it will take some time for your site to rise in search engine rankings. Be wary of any company that promises you instant results as the search engine algorithms do not work instantly.

The SEO company will continue to provide you with content for your website, blog materials, articles, text, video and even photos for your website. You can choose from a variety of different plans. You should not think that this will be something that you can forget about, either. You have to continue to keep up with your website in order to maintain high rankings in the search engines.

By paying attention to search engine optimization, you can see a huge improvement when it comes to traffic that comes to your website. As 60 percent of traffic to your website will come from the search engines, this is not something that you can afford to ignore.

If you think that the only way you can promote your website is through ads, think again. You can get longer lasting and more intense traffic to your site by using SEO. You should not overlook the power of the search engines when it comes to boosting up your sales and increasing traffic to your website online.

# Chapter 13- Finish Line & Time for Say Good BYE

Thanks for finishing the Book Congratulation!!!! If you read and finish the whole book top to bottom, then I am sure you are on the right track for earning huge money. Maybe you are already making some money. Works hard on the topics we discussed previously, and you will make money. That's my promise to you.

I wish you a very happy online journey. Best of Luck.

www.ingramcontent.com/pod-product-compliance
Lightning Source LLC
Chambersburg PA
CBHW071819200526
45169CB00018B/472